21st
Century
Skills Library

ANIMAL INVADERS
FIRE ANT

Barbara A. Somervill

Cherry Lake Publishing
Ann Arbor, Michigan

CHERRY LAKE
Publishing

Published in the United States of America by Cherry Lake Publishing
Ann Arbor, Michigan
www.cherrylakepublishing.com

Content Adviser: Randy Westbrooks, U.S. Geological Survey

Photo Credits: Cover and pages 1, 6, 13, and 24, Courtesy of USDA APHIS PPQ Archive, USDA APHIS PPQ, www.forestryimages.org; page 4, Courtesy of John Ruberson, University of Georgia, www.forestryimages.org; page 8, ©Patrick Lynch/Alamy; page 14, Courtesy of Peggy Greb, USDA Agricultural Research Service, www.forestryimages. org; page 16, ©Chris Evans, River to River CWMA, www.forestryimages.org; page 19, Courtesy of Murray S. Blum, University of Georgia, www.forestryimages.org; page 23, ©iStockphoto.com/TerryJ

Map by XNR Productions Inc.

Library of Congress Cataloging-in-Publication Data

Somervill, Barbara A.
 Fire ant / Barbara A. Somervill.
  p. cm.—(Animal invaders)
 Includes index.
 ISBN-13: 978-1-60279-328-6
 ISBN-10: 1-60279-328-X
 1. Fire ants—Juvenile literature. I. Title. II. Series.
 QL568.F7.S66 2009
 595.79'6—dc22   2008034554

*Cherry Lake Publishing would like to acknowledge the work of
The Partnership for 21st Century Skills.
Please visit www.21stcenturyskills.org for more information.*

Table of Contents

CHAPTER ONE

FIRE ANTS EVERYWHERE!

Red imported fire ants have caused problems in the United States for several decades.

A family in Tennessee is having a picnic. Ants swarm over the food and onto the legs of the picnickers. These pests are red imported fire ants, and they are vicious. Everyone receives painful stings, and the picnic is a disaster.

On a farm in Texas, a tired dog curls up for a nap in the shade of a cottonwood tree. The dog has picked the wrong spot—right on top of a fire ant mound. The stings are so bad that the dog's owner must take it to a veterinarian for shots to relieve the pain.

In Louisiana, a manager watches as fire ants destroy his nursery business. Fire ants have invaded the plants and trees. A nursery cannot sell plants infested with ants. The business is ruined and thousands of dollars are lost.

A golfer in California hits his ball into the rough. Watch out! The rough's thick grass hides a mound of fire ants. As the golfer leans over to move the grass away

At the University of South Florida, St. Petersburg campus, biology classes are studying fire ants. Experiments with fire ants have uncovered some surprising facts. Researchers have found that young fire ant workers play dead when they are in danger. Fire ants that play dead are four times more likely to survive an attack by enemies than older worker ants. What other experiments do you think might be done with fire ants? What would you want to know about these insects?

Fire ants build mounds in many places. Sometimes they choose sites that put cattle or other livestock in danger.

from his ball, the ants attack. Ouch! The penalty for this bad shot is a painful one—dozens of stings from the ants.

Throughout the southern half of the United States, fire ants are on the move. They are spreading farther into new territories and bringing problems with them. Red imported fire ants are not native to the United States.

They are an **invasive species**. They are also killers. Fire ants kill small animals and birds in the wild. They attack other insects and young reptiles.

Fire ant attacks injure pets and livestock, but people are also at risk. Fire ants sting millions of people every year. At greatest risk from these miniature monsters are infants, toddlers, senior citizens, and people with allergies. People who are very allergic to the fire ant's **venom** may die from these stings.

These invaders are not limited to the backyard or open fields. They build tunnel systems under sidewalks and roadways, in building walls, and under floors. These pests damage air conditioners, telephone equipment, and traffic lights. They have even built mounds inside cars and trucks. Drivers have been attacked while operating their vehicles and suffered serious accidents. No place is safe from fire ants.

CHAPTER TWO

ALL ABOUT FIRE ANTS

Fire ants feed on a small reptile. Scientists are concerned about the threats the ants pose to endangered wildlife.

The United States is home to several different species of fire ants. The most common fire ants are red imported fire ants. Other species include southern or California fire ants, black imported fire ants, and tropical or native fire ants.

The ants that cause the majority of problems in the Southeast are red imported fire ants. They have the most toxic venom. Black imported fire ants came from Uruguay and Argentina and took over small areas of Mississippi and Alabama. Although black fire ants arrived in the United States before the red ones, the red ants quickly pushed their cousins to the side. Southern fire ants can be found from California in the West to the Gulf Coast and into Florida. Tropical fire ants range from South Carolina westward to Texas. They usually nest in rotting wood or in mounds around plants.

Fire ants vary in size within a colony. The larger ants are about the length of pencil erasers. The smaller ants are about half as big. The ant is dark reddish brown in color and has a three-part body. The head has **antennae** with clubs on the end. The **abdomen** bears a stinger that delivers venom. The sting is used to defend the ant colony. One ant can sting repeatedly.

Fire ants are **omnivores**. They eat both plants and meat. They commonly feed on ground-nesting animals such as mice. Generally, fire ants prefer the protein of meat, but they also eat trees, seedlings, plants, bulbs and roots, fruits, and grass.

Fire ants live in colonies that build dome-shaped mounds. The mounds may grow quite large. A single colony can have 100,000 to 500,000 fire ants.

Ant colonies are highly organized social structures. Within the colony, every ant has a job. One very important ant is the queen, and fire ant colonies may have several queens. Queens have only one task—to produce eggs. A queen may live 2 to 7 years and produce up to 1,500 eggs every day.

Young fire ants help the queen deliver the eggs. As the eggs develop into **larvae**, the young workers feed the larvae. Other workers are in charge of mound maintenance. They keep the tunnels clean and dig new ones as the colony grows. Older workers head out of the mound in search of food. Guard ants protect the mound from invaders by stinging any creatures that try to enter.

When the mound becomes too crowded, the colony divides itself. When this happens, winged males and females fly into the air to mate. These winged ants are called reproductives. Mating usually takes place at a height of 300 to 800 feet (91 to 244 m) on a warm spring or summer day.

Every fire ant's life begins as an egg. The eggs are small and white. **Unfertilized** eggs can develop into winged males that mate with queens. **Fertilized** eggs will develop into female fire ants.

Red imported fire ant pupae are white. They become darker as they develop.

Once they hatch, eggs develop into larvae, which are white and wormlike. After a few days, the larvae develop into **pupae**. Over time, the pupae develop into mature, adult ants.

It takes about 30 days for a fire ant to develop from an egg to an adult ant. Once they mature, workers live about 6 months. The constant supply of eggs means that there are always larvae, pupae, and adults in the colony.

CHAPTER THREE

HERE COME THE ANTS

Experts examine a red imported fire ant mound. The size of a mound can depend on the type of soil used to form it.

Fire ants are native to Brazil and Argentina, countries in South America. However, they are not usually considered pests there as they are in North America and elsewhere.

Why do fire ants cause trouble in North America? The difference may be that fire ants have natural enemies in

South America. These natural enemies include insects, mammals, and reptiles that eat fire ants. Unfortunately, these enemies did not come along with fire ants when the ants were introduced into North America. So in North America, almost nothing stops the ants from spreading—except for humans!

The arrival of fire ants in North America was not a planned invasion. The ants were stowaways. At first, no one knew they had arrived. No one knows for sure how the fire ants were introduced. They may have been hidden in imported lumber, the soil of potted plants, or ships' **ballast** soil.

Scientists now believe that there were two separate fire ant invasions. The first ants to arrive were black imported fire ants from Argentina (*Solenopsis richteri*). They probably came sometime around 1918 and spread quickly. But they were a minor problem compared to the next ants to arrive. Those were red imported fire ants

Their aggressive behavior has helped fire ants successfully invade many parts of the world.

(*Solenopsis invicta*). They arrived at the port of Mobile, Alabama, in the 1930s. The red imported fire ants took over, pushing aside their black cousins.

So far, the only barrier for the fire ants is climate. Most fire ants cannot survive in areas where the ground freezes for months at a time in winter. It is possible, however, for fire ants to move north as stowaways. They could infest

potted plants that are shipped from southern states northward. Once in the North, the ants would look for a warm place to build a new nest, such as in a steam pipe, under a building, or in a wall. If the ants find a warm environment for a mound, they will survive in the North.

Since the arrival of fire ants in the United States, the invaders have spread worldwide. Red imported fire ants are now found in Asian and Pacific countries, including China, Taiwan, and Malaysia. In 2001, red imported fire ants were accidentally introduced into Queensland, Australia.

The fire ant problem is so serious that the United Nations held a meeting to discuss how to contain the insects.

"The problem is enormous—far bigger than people had previously thought," said Sarah Simons, Executive Director of the Global Invasive Species Programme (GISP) in Nairobi, Kenya.

Fire ants can destroy young plants. They injure pets, livestock, and wildlife. They munch their way through wires on equipment, causing as much as several billion dollars worth of damage a year in the United States alone. It doesn't take many ants to start an ant invasion. All that is needed is a queen and a mate. Once a fire ant queen starts producing eggs, the invasion is under way.

CHAPTER FOUR

PROBLEMS WITH FIRE ANTS

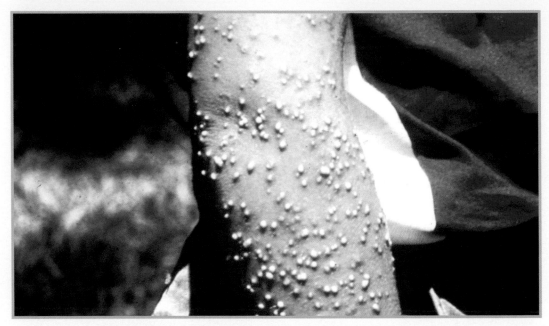

Red imported fire ants are fiercely defensive. A person who disturbs a fire ant mound may receive many painful stings.

Individual fire ants are tiny, but the problems they cause are huge. Fire ants affect humans and animals. They also disrupt the balance of nature. Fire ants are costly pests that are out of control.

Some people might say, "So we can't have a picnic—big deal." But it is a big deal. Recreation is an important human activity. Many people earn a living providing recreation services. They tend the grass on golf courses or maintain public parks. And recreation is only one area where fire ants cause problems.

The medical costs of caring for people with fire ant bites can be high. A trip to the emergency room, medicine, and a follow-up visit to the doctor's office can cost hundreds of dollars or more. Thousands of such cases occur each year. While not all people require a doctor's visit, many do buy over-the-counter medicines to relieve the sting and itching. The costs of these medicines may add up to millions of dollars each year.

A 2007 study in Texas figured out the costs of red imported fire ants in the state.

Some **endangered** species are being affected by the fire ant invasion. In the Florida Keys, researchers have discovered that fire ants feed on sea turtle eggs and attack Lower Keys marsh rabbits and Stock Island tree snails. **Conservationists** need to be flexible in their thinking so they can balance two often conflicting priorities—getting rid of the invasive species while still protecting the endangered species.

Farmers estimate that fire ant damage costs an average of $1,691 per farm. Across the entire state, damage estimates mount up to about $236.5 million. Among the farm products affected are cotton, grain, timber, hay, sheep, goats, beef cattle, and poultry. Fire ants can damage farm buildings, houses, roads, cars, and trucks.

Fire ants eat plants. They have destroyed many crops by feeding on sprouts, roots, fruits, or seeds. Among the crops damaged by fire ants are corn, okra, strawberries, pecans, and potatoes. Fire ants also damage citrus trees by chewing on the bark.

Fire ants have even caused large sections of highways to collapse. The ants shift large amounts of soil as they tunnel under the roads. They build huge tunnel networks under the asphalt, and the road simply caves in. This is very dangerous for motorists who assume a road is safe.

Within homes, no place is safe from invading fire ants. They particularly like electrical appliances and have been found nesting in televisions, air conditioners, and water heaters. They will also invade plumbing fixtures, carpet, and the insulation between walls. Fire ants will even nest in laundry.

Fire ants have invaded more than 300 million acres (121 million hectares) of land in the southern United States and in Puerto Rico. When invasive species such as fire ants are introduced into an ecosystem, they throw off the balance of nature. In every ecosystem, **predators** and prey, animals and plants, all live in balance.

Animal invaders usually do not have natural predators to control them in a new country. In the United States,

Armadillos are one type of animal that preys on fire ants.

armadillos are one type of animal that feeds on fire ants. But armadillos are not enough to keep the fire ants under control. So fire ants continue to spread.

Whether humans realize it or not, they also depend on nature's balance to live. They depend on crops for food and the timber from forests for building. Changes in nature's cycle of life impact everyone.

CHAPTER FIVE

IS THERE ANY SOLUTION?

Bait is one weapon against fire ants. The best defense plans include a combination of different ways to attack and control the invaders.

The war on fire ants began in the 1950s. So far, the ants are winning. In the 1960s, the federal government tried spraying from the air, using highly poisonous **pesticides**. The chemicals did kill some fire ants, but their use had a more serious effect on pets, cattle, birds, fish, and raccoons. In some states, the bird population dropped significantly because of the spraying. The program wasted more than $70 million. When it ended, the fire ants had spread from 90 million to 133 million acres (36 million to 54 million ha).

Another effort to stop the spread of fire ants is the inspection of hay, soil-moving equipment, sod, and potted plants from infected areas. That seems like a good idea, but it is not completely successful either. The ants develop new colonies by flying to find new homes. They can fly a maximum of only 10 miles (16 km), but they can start new colonies several times a year if necessary.

Many households, farms, businesses, and government agencies have tried to solve the problem of fire ants. More than 100 chemical products have been developed for killing fire ants. Most are poisoned baits that work reasonably well. The problem is that even if the bait kills most of the fire ants in a mound, some ants will survive. New queens will emerge, thousands of eggs a day will be produced, and in less than a year, the colony will be strong again.

One natural enemy of fire ants is the phorid fly. The effectiveness of the flies in getting rid of fire ants is being researched. In South America, 20 species of phorid flies are effective in controlling fire ants. Two species of these small humpbacked flies, which resemble fruit flies, have been introduced into the United States.

This is how phorid flies work: A female phorid fly hovers around a fire ant mound, looking for the perfect host. When that host is found, the fly dive-bombs the fire ant and injects an egg into its body.

Within 10 days, the fly larva has killed the host ant. It thrives in the ant mound and develops into an adult phorid fly. The flies usually choose worker ants as hosts for their young. This not only kills the ants, but it also limits the number of ants that can search for food. The

ants go into hiding when they sense the presence of the flies, which further limits the ants' hunting.

So why don't we use phorid flies to combat the fire ant invasion in the United States? Phorid flies may not be enough to control the infestation of fire ants in the United States today. Also, introducing phorid flies where they don't belong could create an invasive fly problem. Further study of the flies is needed.

Research into the possibility of killing fire ants by flooding nests with water hasn't been successful. But it has uncovered a very interesting fire ant behavior. To keep from drowning, the entire ant colony forms itself into a ball, sometimes as large as a basketball. The water rises and the ball of ants floats on top, constantly rolling so that all the ants can breathe. As soon as the ant ball hits something solid, the ants climb aboard and begin reestablishing their colony.

Throughout the southern states where fire ants live, billions of dollars have been lost through crop and building damage. A lot of money has been spent on research and chemical products to kill the ants. So far, the money, time, and effort spent have not reduced the fire ant population in the United States at all.

Fire ants continue to spread into new areas. In California, the Department of Food and Agriculture says that "the possibility of eradication is low and will be difficult to achieve." It looks like the fire ant is one invasive species that is here to stay.

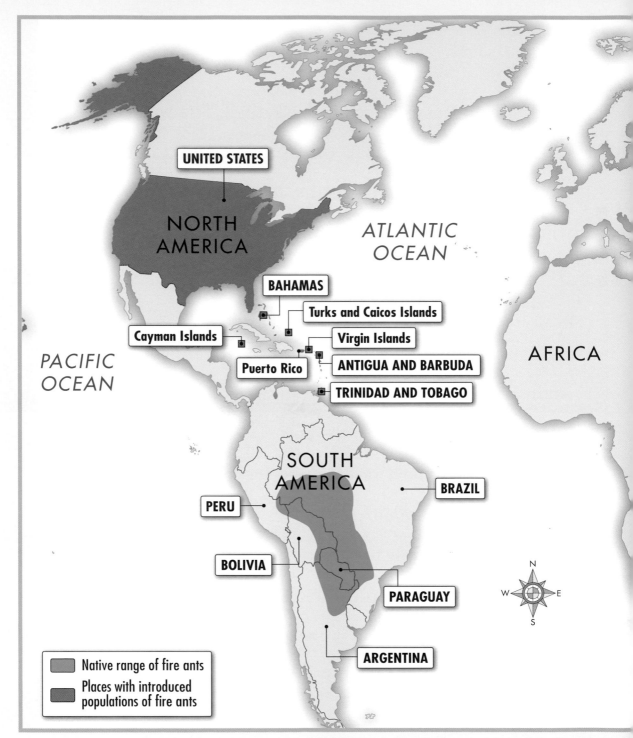

UNITED STATES

NORTH
AMERICA

ATLANTIC
OCEAN

BAHAMAS

Turks and Caicos Islands

Cayman Islands

PACIFIC
OCEAN

Virgin Islands

Puerto Rico

ANTIGUA AND BARBUDA

TRINIDAD AND TOBAGO

AFRICA

SOUTH
AMERICA

BRAZIL

PERU

BOLIVIA

PARAGUAY

ARGENTINA

N
W — E
S

Native range of fire ants

Places with introduced
populations of fire ants

This map shows where in the world the red imported

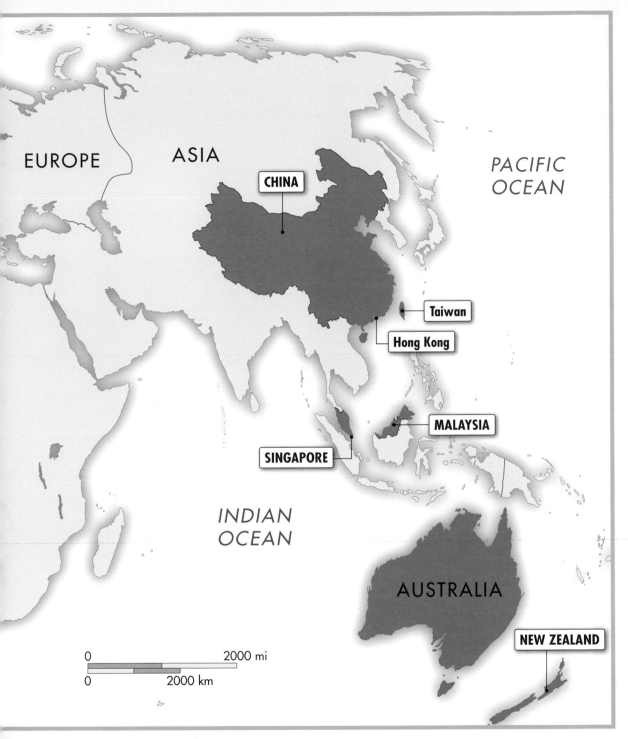

EUROPE

ASIA

PACIFIC
OCEAN

CHINA

Taiwan

Hong Kong

MALAYSIA

SINGAPORE

INDIAN
OCEAN

AUSTRALIA

NEW ZEALAND

0   2000 mi

0   2000 km

fire ant lives naturally and where it has invaded.

Glossary

abdomen (AB-duh-muhn) the back section of an insect's body

antennae (an-TEN-ee) feelers on an insect's head

ballast (BA-lust) something heavy that is placed in a ship to improve stability and control

conservationists (kon-sur-VAY-shuhn-ists) people who work to preserve, manage, and care for the environment

endangered (ehn-DAYN-jurd) at risk of dying out completely

fertilized (FUR-tuh-lized) having had male and female reproductive cells united

invasive species (in-VAY-siv SPEE-sheez) any plant or animal that is not native to an area but has moved into the region

larvae (LAR-vee) immature insects that look like worms

omnivores (OM-nuh-vorz) animals that eat both meat and plants

pesticides (PESS-tuh-sides) chemical substances designed to kill pests such as rats, mice, or insects

predators (PRED-uh-turz) animals that hunt and kill other animals for food

pupae (PYOO-pee) insects at the stage between being larvae and adults

unfertilized (uhn-FUR-tuh-lized) a state in which a female reproductive cell does not become united with a male reproductive cell

venom (VEN-uhm) poison produced by some insects and other animals

For More Information

Books

Lockwood, Sophie. *Ants*. Mankato, MN: The Child's World, 2008.

Souza, D. M., and Jack Harris (illustrator). *Packed with Poison! Deadly Animal Defenses*. Minneapolis: Millbrook Press, 2006.

Web Sites

Featured Creatures: Red Imported Fire Ant
creatures.ifas.ufl.edu/urban/ants/red_imported_fire_ant.htm
See photographs and read information about this vicious fire ant species

Hey! A Fire Ant Stung Me!
kidshealth.org/kid/ill_injure/bugs/fire_ant.html
To learn more about what to do if you are stung by fire ants

INDEX

ABOUT THE AUTHOR

Barbara A. Somervill writes children's nonfiction books on a variety of topics. As a writer, she has had many different cool careers—teacher, news reporter, author, scriptwriter, and restaurant critic. She believes that researching new and different topics makes writing every book an adventure. When she is not writing, Ms. Somervill plays duplicate bridge, reads avidly, and travels.